# Of picnic

Written by
Tapasi De

Illustrated by
Suman S. Roy

Our summer holidays were about to begin. We were all very happy.

Our teacher Ms Jennifer said that we would go for a picnic before the school closed.

We were all excited. We asked our teacher where we would go.

Lily said that we should go to a place where there was a lake.

But David said that boys would like to go to a forest.

Some others thought that we should go to an amusement park.

Ms Jennifer said that she knew a place which all the children would like.

She said that we should go to the countryside where there was a lake, hills and lots of trees.

We all liked the idea. And so, Ms Jennifer took permission from the Principal.

The next day, Ms Jennifer divided us into groups. She told us to bring different things for the picnic.

Each group had to bring ground mats, food, drinks and toys.

Finally, the day of the picnic arrived. We all gathered in school.

At 10 o' clock we left from school in a big bus. On the way, we sang and recited poems.

An hour later, we reached the countryside. It was green all around. The air was fresh.

There was a big, blue lake. The water looked cool and deep.

We quickly got into our groups. In my group there was Susie, Harry, Alina and Jerry.

The sun shone brightly. Ms Jennifer said that we could have our drinks if we wished to.

After this, we began to play. Ms Jennifer and Ms Anne watched us play.

Some played chasing games and some played with the ball.

We wanted to go boating in the lake. But Ms Jennifer said it could be dangerous.

After sometime, our teachers called us. We all sat in a big circle.

Ms Anne said that each of us would do something. We sang, danced, recited and told stories!

We were surprised to see that we could do so many things! We felt so proud of ourselves.

At 2 o' clock we had our lunch. We had noodles, sandwiches, hot dogs and fruits.

We even shared our food with the other groups. We had never eaten such a variety of food, ever.

After lunch, we cleaned the place and gathered the litter. We packed our things in the picnic baskets.

After lunch we sat and shared a thing or two about ourselves. We even clicked photographs.

Finally, it was time to go home. We all boarded the bus and began our journey back.

When we reached our school, it was evening. It was nice to see our school at night.

Our parents were waiting for us. We all went back happy but a little tired.

# Let's spell new words

| | |
|---|---|
| holidays | Principal |
| vacations | enjoyable |
| picnic | countryside |
| discussing | ground mats |
| excited | permission |
| amusement | travelling |
| park | clicked |
| classmate | photographs |
| adventure | |
| forest | |
| permission | |